CORRECT THE
10 MOST
COMMON
GOLF PROBLEMS IN
10 DAYS

CORRECT THE 10 MOST COMMON GOLF PROBLEMS IN 10 DAYS

Walter Ostroske
PGA Teaching Pro

and John Devaney

Photography by Aime La Montagne

A PERIGEE BOOK

Perigee Books
are published by
The Putnam Publishing Group
200 Madison Avenue
New York, NY 10016

Library of Congress Cataloging-in-Publication Data

Ostroske, Walter.
     Correct the 10 most common golf problems in 10 days / by Walter
Ostroske and John Devaney; photography by Aime La Montagne.
          p.   cm.
     "A Perigee book."
     ISBN 0-399-51656-5 (alk. paper)
     1. Golf.   I. Devaney, John.   II. Title.   III. Title: Correct the
ten most common golf problems in ten days.
GV965.O58   1991   90-22959   CIP
796.352—dc20

Cover design © 1991
  by Richard Rossiter
Cover photograph © 1991
  by Aime La Montagne

Printed in the United States of America

8   9   10

This book is printed on acid-free paper.

This book is dedicated to my favorite foursome:
Paige, Kevin, Danielle, and Kimberly—my children.
                                              —W.O.

And to all those golfers who ask after an errant shot,
"Hey, somebody, tell me what I'm doing wrong."
                                              —J.D.

Contents

The Golf Clinic

A 10-DAY CHECKUP CAN SHAVE 10 OR MORE STROKES OFF YOUR GAME

Golf pros are like medical doctors in many ways. People come to us and complain that there is something sick about their swing. I'll watch hackers as well as low-handicappers swing for ten or fifteen minutes. In that time I will see the symptoms of their problems, make a diagnosis of why they are making those mistakes, and decide on remedies to cure the problems. Then I'll give the golfers a clinical session. We work head to head on doing right what they have been doing wrong. Finally, I'll send them away with a prescription for how to work alone to erase *permanently* those errors from their games.

I have spent much of the past twenty-five years showing weekenders—men and women who play no more than fifteen or twenty times a year, mostly on weekends—that those golfing woes fatten their scores because they are committing one or all of the ten most common golf errors. Those problems cause a low-handicapper to miss a target by ten yards, a high-handicapper to miss it by thirty or forty yards. (Problems that have become contagious can cause you to miss the ball altogether!) For both

9

the high- and low-handicapper, those errors keep you from breaking 100, 90, or 80.

Give me one day for correcting each of these problems. I ask that you first read how to correct each error. Then practice for an hour each day, at a range, at a course, or at home in your living room or backyard. After ten days you are going to make those mistakes less often or not at all. And when one of those ten common mistakes creeps back into your swing, you will know what's wrong and how to go about getting rid of it. Along the way, you are going to see a 100 golfer becoming a 90 golfer, a 90 golfer becoming an 80 or even a high-70s golfer.

What are the ten most common golf errors?

1) A faulty grip and position over the ball.
2) Swinging too hard from the tee.
3) Swinging down and around instead of down and through.
4) Leaving the approach shot short of the green.
5) Going from trouble to more trouble.
6) Failing to make the ends match when you putt.
7) Shifting your weight the wrong way.
8) "Slow-Smash" rhythm and tempo.
9) Choosing the wrong club for par-3 tee shots.
10) Slicing.

I have always maintained that golf is a simple game: Bring the club up, bring the club down, bring the club through. *Swing through* the ball, don't *hit at* it. When you execute a proper golf swing, the ball just happens to get in the way of the clubhead. So if golf is a simple game, then correcting these ten faults should be just as simple.

That's the all-important mechanical side of golf. There's also a mental side of golf, like knowing how to play a dogleg the comfortable way or the hard way. Here, too, I see weekenders making mistakes that cost them strokes. As part of our clinic, I'll tell you how to get rid of the most critical mental mistakes that I see golfers making most often.

TONING UP

This practice session will impress into your muscle memory the interaction of the arms and shoulders (what I call the upper gear) with the hips, legs, and knees (the lower gear) during a proper golf swing.

Stand in front of a mirror. Place a ball directly in the center of your shoulder-width stance. Put both hands on your hips. Turn to your right until the left elbow and the left hip and the left knee are pointing directly at the ball. You are simulating a proper upswing. Then turn to your left until the right elbow and the right hip and the right knee are pointing directly at the ball. You are simulating a proper downswing and follow-through. And you are getting the feeling of a golf swing, not a golf hit.

Now let's start with Day One.

DAY ONE

A Faulty Grip and Position over the Ball

A FAULTY GRIP

SYMPTOMS: Hooks to the left or slices to the right, as well as straight shots that always go far left or far right of the target.

DIAGNOSIS: The left hand (or the right hand in the case of lefty golfers) is placed too far over on the shaft. This occurs when you grasp the shaft from the bottom or the top. If the left hand comes at the shaft from the top, it will be too strong and you will close the clubface at impact, causing the ball to hook or go straight but left of the target. If the left hand comes at the shaft from the bottom, you will open the clubface at impact, causing the ball to slice or at best go straight but to the right of the target.

REMEDY: Learn the proper way to grip a club. Grasp the shaft from the sides—not from the top, not from

The left hand is placed too far over on the shaft because the golfer approached the shaft with his hands from the top or the bottom.

A closed clubface will cause the ball to hook.

An open clubface will cause the ball to slice.

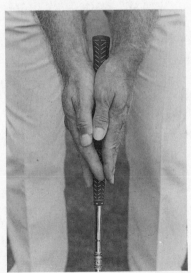

The palms of the hands come together in a praying position with the clubshaft happening to get in their way.

15

the bottom. Bring the palms of your hands together in a position of prayer so that the clubshaft happens to get in the way of the palms.

LET'S GO TO THE CLINIC: Here's what I see many high-handicappers do when they grip a club: One palm is facing the sky, the other is facing the ground. You can't guide or control a clubhead with the hands positioned in that manner—in effect, at right angles to the projected line of flight.

Both hands must be working in synch. That means *both palms must face each other.* Pick up a club and place it so that its grip is leaning against your midsection. Now bring both hands together from the sides so that they come together as though you were clapping hands around the grip. Now, all you have to do is slide one hand upward (the left if you are a righty), the other hand downward—and believe it or not—you have a proper golf grip.

It is not a finely tuned grip, but the hands are positioned the way they should be for hitting a straight shot. The back of the left hand faces the target, the back of the right hand faces a point behind you that is on a straight line with the target.

To fine-tune the grip, I recommend the overlapping or Vardon grip. As we described in our previous book, *Break 100 in 21 Days*, this is how you apply the fingers in the overlapping grip:

Your left thumb points straight down the shaft to the clubface. Your thumb and forefinger grip the

Correct! The back of the left hand faces the target, the back of the right hand faces a point behind you that is on a straight line with the target.

The overlapping grip: The left thumb points straight down the shaft toward the clubhead . . .

. . . the right hand covers the left thumb; the right thumb points straight down the shaft toward the clubhead.

club very lightly. The last three fingers of the left hand, however, grip the club very, very firmly. These are the guiding and supporting fingers.

The right hand covers the left thumb. The little pinky of the right hand, which isn't strong enough to go around the shaft, lies on top of the left hand. The right thumb points straight down the shaft. The thumb and forefinger grip the club very, very firmly. The other three fingers hold the club lightly.

This grip, with the back of the left hand pointing at the target at impact, is the grip that will keep the clubhead tracing the same arc coming down as the one it traced going up. And this grip will keep the clubhead square to the target line as you bring the club into the impact area.

Here are two questions I am frequently asked about the grip:

1. How tightly should I grip the club?

Most golfers tend to grip the club too tightly. It has been said that you shouldn't squeeze the club so tightly that you'd strangle a small bird if you had a bird instead of a club in your hands. I like to put it this way: You should hold the club firmly so that the clubhead will not move when it impacts the ball or the ground.

Determine if you have that kind of solid grip with this test: Grip the club as you usually do. Hold the clubhead out so that a friend can try to turn it left or right. The friend should not be able to turn the clubhead.

A friend should not be able to turn the clubhead if you are gripping it properly.

Remember: Hold the club but don't squeeze it.

2. Where do I put my hands on the grip?

Never grip a wood or an iron at the very end. Only the putter is gripped at the end with no shaft showing (so you can get a full pendulum-like swing). When you hold a wood or an iron, some shaft should show above your hands—from a half to three-quarters of an inch. If you grip the shaft at the end, the weight of the clubhead at the top of your backswing will put too much pressure on the fleshy outside pad of your left hand. That may give you a blister, for one thing, and a wayward shot, for another. When you grip the shaft at the end, there is likely to be "play," or looseness, in the grip at the top of the backswing—that is, at the point when the club is parallel to the ground. That looseness will cause the clubhead to open or close as you bring it into the impact area, resulting in a hook or a slice.

Gripping the shaft at the end will put too much pressure on the fleshy pad of your left hand, causing blisters. Some shaft should show above your grip.

PRESCRIPTION:

1) At home or in the backyard, extend your arms straight out at your sides. Bring both palms together slowly so that they meet at a point directly between your eyes, and clap the palms together. Do this at least two dozen times, clapping your palms so that they meet each time at exactly the same point between your eyes. Make sure that neither the right nor the left overpowers the other. They should clap together with the same force each time.

2) Now place a club on the ground so that the grip rests against your midsection. Practice bringing both hands toward the grip from the sides, forming a position of prayer with the shaft in between them. The palm of the right hand is facing 180 degrees toward the target, the palm of the left hand is facing a point 180 degrees away from the target. Then let go of the club so that the grip falls against your abdomen. Again, without looking down, let your hands come together from the sides so that they grasp the shaft with the palms facing each other.

3) Bring both palms together from the sides so they meet with the grip in between them. Slide the left hand up and the right hand down. Point the left thumb so that it is facing the backswing area, point the right thumb so that it is facing the target area.

Practice all three of these exercises while placing

the fingers correctly for the overlapping grip (as shown on page 18) without looking down at your hands. After an hour or so of doing those three drills, the correct grip should feel as familiar to you as a handshake with a friend.

A FAULTY POSITION OVER THE BALL

SYMPTOMS: Shots that go off line to the left; pop-fly shots from the tee with the driver and from the fairway with woods or long irons.

DIAGNOSIS: The golfer is standing so far away from the ball that he or she must bend at the waist at close to a 45-degree angle to reach it. The golfer is bending at the waist instead of inclining at the waist and bending at the knees. As a result, to reach the ball, the golfer makes a down-and-around swing like a baseball slugger instead of a down-and-up golf swing.

REMEDY: Stand close enough to the ball so that you need only bend at the knees—while inclining at the waist—to reach the ball.

LET'S GO TO THE CLINIC: Start with this basic: When you address the ball, *bend at the knees*, forming a half-sitting position. *Don't bend at the waist* to such a

Wrong! Bending at the waist induces a down-and-around swing.

Correct! Bend the knees, incline the waist.

degree that your back is tilted more than 30 degrees.

Now I am going to answer two questions that will set you straight on how far you should stand from the ball, and where the ball should be placed for every shot you will ever take.

1) How do I know I am standing the right distance from the ball?

Place a ball on the ground and step toward it with a club in your hands. Address the ball as you would normally, but place your feet so close to the ball that they are almost touching it. Your forearms will be pushing against your body. Your arms and hands will be too confined to swing the club.

Now shuffle back a few inches. Keep on shuffling back until your arms are no longer touching your body and you have room for your arms and hands to pass in front of you. You are standing the correct distance from the ball when your arms, hands, and club have enough space to comfortably pass your body without touching it. When you stand at address, there should be enough space for your outstretched right hand to pass between the top of the club and your right thigh.

2) Where do I place the ball in relation to my feet?

Older golf books taught you to place the ball in the middle of your stance—that is, smack between both feet—for the middle irons like the 5 and 6; you were told to move the ball back toward your

At address there should be enough space for the hand to pass between shaft and thigh.

right foot as you went to shorter irons like the 7 and 8; you were told to move the ball forward toward your front foot when you swung the longer clubs like the 3- and 4-iron or the fairway woods.

That advice is out the window as far as I am concerned. Why? Because all weekenders, high-handicappers and low-handicappers, must take pretty much the same swing for all shots. They don't have the time to practice different swings for different clubs or lies.

What this means: Put the ball in the same spot for all shots from the fairway—and that spot is in the middle of your stance. You want to hit downward on these shots to get the ball up in the air. When the ball is placed in the middle of the stance, the clubhead will catch the ball on the down part of the swing—just before the bottom of the arc.

But when the ball is already in the air—when it is teed up for a shot with a driver or an iron on a par-3 hole—you no longer need that downward blow to get the ball up in the air. The ball is already up in the air. Now you need a sweeping shot that will catch the ball on the upward arc of the swing. So place the ball a few inches forward of center so that it is about opposite the left heel.

Similarly, when you blast a ball out of sand, you want to catch the ball after impact on the upswing to make sure the ball gets up and out. So, when blasting out of sand, place the ball a few inches forward, just about opposite the left heel. (There is

On the fairway the ball is placed in the middle of the stance so the clubhead catches the ball just before the bottom of the swing.

On the tee the ball is placed forward of center, opposite the left heel, so that the clubhead will catch the ball on the upward arc of the swing.

an exception to this rule when in sand, which I will explain later on when we talk about getting in and out of trouble spots.)

To sum up: 1) Stand close enough to the ball so that you need to bend only at the knees and not at the waist, with the shaft no more than about a hand's length away from your right thigh. 2) The ball is always placed in the middle of the stance except when it's teed up, or when you are blasting out of a greenside bunker. Then it's placed slightly forward, about opposite the left heel.

PRESCRIPTION: Place a ball in the middle of your stance. Assuming the proper grip, place the clubhead directly on top of the ball. Now raise the clubhead over your head just as though you were swinging an axe to chop a log. You will have to bend your elbows as you bring the clubhead back over your head. Now bring the clubhead down toward the ball, straightening out the arms as they were at address. Bring the clubhead back to where it was at address—directly over the ball.

This drill stresses to your muscle memory that the proper (and comfortable) position for you is one where you only have to incline your back slightly (while bending the knees) to reach the ball. And it also makes you feel natural about having the ball in the middle of your stance for all of your fairway shots.

DAY TWO

Swinging Too Hard from the Tee

SYMPTOMS: Drives that veer left or right into the rough or out of bounds; drives that cut through grass or soar sky-high.

DIAGNOSIS: The downswing is at least twice as fast as the upswing.

REMEDY: Slow down the downswing so that it is as close to the speed of the upswing as possible; fully extend your arms during the follow-through.

LET'S GO TO THE CLINIC: I am always a little surprised when I see how many golfers refuse to trust their drivers. Drivers have been crafted to do a specific job: drive the ball a long distance. The driver has the longest shaft of any club in your bag. It also has the biggest clubhead of any club in your bag. The driver has a minimum degree of loft to provide distance rather than height. It is a long-distance weapon that asks only one thing from you: "Get me to a ball with a proper golf swing and I will do the rest."

But too many golfers think this way: "I am at the tee and as far away from the pin as I can be. Therefore, I need distance. So I will swing this driver as fast and as hard as I can to get the most distance."

In fact, the reverse is true: To get maximum distance with a distance club like the driver, you must swing the club slow and easy, not hard and fast. True, you need clubhead speed for distance off a tee, but you won't get clubhead speed by swinging the club faster on the downswing.

Let me explain what I mean. Since the driver has the longest shaft of any club in your bag, the arc in your swing—both on the backswing and on the follow-through—should be wider than that in a swing with any other club. And it is that wide arc in the downswing that produces clubhead speed— the speed that gives maximum distance.

So—listen to this carefully—it is not the speed you add to the downswing that gives true clubhead speed; it is the widest possible arc on the upswing and the downswing that gives you clubhead speed.

To ensure that you get that wide arc on the backswing, you must take the club back slowly, making sure that all the pieces of the swing are fitting together: The shoulders turn, the arms extend back and up, the wrists cock, the hands maintain a firm grip at the top of the backswing. Because the swing with the driver is so wide and full, and be-

As I am showing here, the arc of the driver's backswing is wider than the arc of a swing with any other club.

cause this swing has such a wide arc—the length of the driver's shaft plus the length of your arms—it is important on the backswing that you take your time and make sure that all the pieces come together in the proper sequence.

Now it is true that most golfers take their time on the backswing. They go back at thirty miles per hour. But then they tell themselves they have to whack that little rascal as hard as they can to get maximum distance. They come down at sixty miles per hour. And the pieces that came together so neatly on the backswing now come apart during the downswing because they don't have time to come together.

Here is what can happen:

If an arm doesn't straighten, for example, the arc of the downswing is not fully extended. Result: The arc is not as wide as it should be and you lose clubhead speed. Or if the hands are in front of the clubhead, there is no late release of the wrists, and that takes all the zing and fire out of the shot.

What has a speeded-up downswing done for you so far? It has taken away clubhead speed and that costs you distance. And if you don't take the time to straighten your arms at impact, you are likely to catch the top of the ball and get no loft on the shot. You'll top it and get a grass cutter or maybe miss it altogether. Or you'll catch the ball on the bottom and get one of those sky-high pop-ups.

Too quick a downswing can leave you in worse

If the hands are in front of the clubhead just before impact, there is no uncocking (or snapping) of the wrists and, as a result, no zing to the shot.

places than short off the tee. If, during the rush coming down to impact, the arms stay bent, the clubhead will meet the ball with either an open face (a slice) or a closed face (a hook). A hook or a slice out of bounds will cost you both distance and a penalty stroke.

Now let's do it right from the tee. Take the clubhead back *and* up very slowly, turning the shoulders and extending the arms fully to get that wide arc from the long shaft. Bring the club down as closely as possible to the speed of the upswing. If it went up at thirty-five miles per hour, it should come down at no more than forty miles per hour. Make sure that you maintain that wide arc on the downswing—the same arc you traced on the way up. Make sure that the wrists uncock—the so-called "late release"—so that the clubhead moves ahead of the hands just before impact. Make sure that at impact the arms form the same "V" that they formed at address.

That covers the downswing of the tee shot, which is where I see high-handicappers and low-handicappers making their big mistake—swinging down too fast.

But I see other golfers make another mistake during the follow-through with a driver. Their arms are not fully extended during the follow-through and thus they fail to take full advantage of the length of the driver's shaft. They do not get as wide an arc during the follow-through as they got during the backswing.

Again, keep in mind that the swing arc with the driver is wider than with any other club because of the length of the driver's shaft. That means more clubhead speed than with any other club. To get the maximum clubhead speed and put "send" on your tee shots, you must extend your arms out toward the target during the follow-through and maintain that wide arc. You must also maintain those V-shaped arms until the hands come past the belt buckle. Then the arms begin to collapse as the clubhead finishes up *above*—not around—the shoulders.

Keep the follow-through in mind when hitting from the tee. When you hit from the fairway, the ball is on the ground. You must concentrate on a downswing that lifts the ball up. That should take about 50 percent of your effort; the other 50 percent should be used in getting the ball to go a specific distance, depending on the club.

But when you hit from the tee, the ball is already in the air! So you need only 40 percent of your effort on the downswing. The other 60 percent should go into the follow-through, keeping the arms fully extended in a W-I-D-E, W-I-D-E arc. That wide arc in the follow-through—the arms fully extended toward the target—will add "send" to your drives while ensuring that the ball will go to your target area.

PRESCRIPTION: Pick up a driver and grip it by the clubhead. Swing the club for fifteen minutes. Since there is no

To put "send" on your tee shots, maintain the V-shaped arms during the follow-through until the hands pass the belt buckle.

Wrong! The clubhead should not finish around the shoulders.

It should finish above the shoulders.

A drill to give you the sensation of a paced swing in which the speed of the downswing matches the speed of the upswing: Grip the club by the neck and swing with only the left arm, continuing to a full finish as you bring the right side of your body around.

weight at the end of the club, you will tend to execute a downswing that is about the same speed as your upswing. There is no temptation to bring the club down quickly. Practice this as often as you can and you will get the feeling of a perfect golf swing—a swing that is thirty-five miles per hour on the way up and thirty-five miles per hour on the way down.

Then do a second exercise for another fifteen minutes:

Assume the stance for a tee shot with both hands on the grip. Then take the right hand away from the driver and place it on your right thigh. Using only the left arm, bring the club back in a full takeaway until you reach the top of the backswing, the left shoulder touching the chin. With the left shoulder and the left hip turning, bring the club down with only the left arm and continue the swing to a full finish as you bring the right side of your body around. When you are forced to swing with only the left arm (the right if you are a lefty), you can't swing the club too fast or with too much force. You will get the sensation of a true, paced golf swing.

DAY THREE

Swinging Down and Around with the Fairway Woods and Irons

SYMPTOMS: Hooks to the left as well as straight shots that consistently land to the left of the target.

DIAGNOSIS: The left arm is "quitting" at impact.

REMEDY: The left arm must work "overtime."

LET'S GO TO THE CLINIC: Here's a common scenario: When a golfer hits from the fairway, he or she is thinking primarily of distance. The golfer wants to gobble up yardage to get close to the green for a favorite short-iron shot.

So what happens? The golfer puts all of his or her force and energy into the downswing. Since most people are right-handed, that means the right hand and the right side overpower the left hand and the

43

left side. When the right side overpowers the left, one of two things happens and both are bad:

1. The overpowering right side causes the clubhead to come across the line of flight instead of continuing in the line of flight. As a result, the clubhead is closed when it impacts the ball. The closed clubface causes a hooking spin that sends the ball curving to the golfer's left.

2. The overpowering right side causes the body to turn too soon before impact; that brings the left shoulder around too soon. Again the clubhead comes across the line of flight instead of continuing in the line of flight. The clubhead may meet the ball squarely and the ball will go on a straight line. But that straight line is now straight to the left of the target.

The photos on these pages show what I mean. I am coming down with my right side and with my right arm leading the parade. They are ahead of the clubface, which should be leading the parade. The left arm and the left side are being overpowered by the right arm and the right side. So what do they do? They quit at impact and now the right side completely takes over. With the left arm now doing nothing, the result is a follow-through in which the club comes *below* the left shoulder, like a baseball batter's swing. The clubhead should come up and *away* from the body and finish *above* the left shoulder.

My right side and my right arm are ahead of the clubface, which should be leading the parade instead of trailing.

The left arm and left side collapse after impact and the clubhead comes around and below the left shoulder instead of high and above the left shoulder.

I tell golfers to remember that on all fairway shots, whether you are swinging a wood or an iron, to get the ball up the left arm must do 50 percent of the work in bringing the club down. The left arm and left shoulder must also provide at least 50 percent of the effort in bringing the clubhead up and high above the left shoulder. The clubhead must "lead the parade" and should be followed by the left side and then the right side as the clubhead comes up after impact into and through the shaking-hands position of the follow-through.

In short, the left arm and left side put 50 percent of the effort into the downswing and maybe as much as 60 percent of the effort into the follow-through. That adds up to 110 percent because in a good golf swing from the fairway, the left side must work overtime.

PRESCRIPTION: Grip a club by the neck and bring it all the way back and up to the top of the backswing, then bring it down and through to a full and high follow-through with the left arm fully extended and the left arm up and above the shoulder. Practice this for fifteen to thirty minutes. You are swinging without the weight pressure of the clubhead and as a result there is no tendency for the body to come in and help swing that weight. And the wider the arc you trace when you bring the club back and up and then downward, the louder the whooshing sound you are going to make as you come through the impact area. You should hear that whooshing sound in an actual golf swing when the left arm does not quit but continues into a follow-through that is on line with the target.

Grip the club by the grip and take practice swings for fifteen minutes with your feet and legs

47

Practice with the feet and legs close together. This gives the feeling of swinging with only the upper gear and makes the left arm work overtime.

close together. This gives the feeling of swinging with only the arms, hands, and shoulders. It puts more emphasis on a full swing with the left arm working overtime, and it takes out the action of the body.

48

Leaving the Approach Shot Short of the Green

SYMPTOMS: Shots from within 100 to 120 yards of the green that land 10 to 30 yards short and are occasionally off line.

DIAGNOSIS: Selecting too weak a club and then taking too strong a swing.

REMEDY: Select a stronger club than you would normally use for the distance and take a moderate swing.

LET'S GO TO THE CLINIC: You have landed about 100 yards from the green with your second shot on a short par-4 hole. Now you need only land the ball anywhere on the green and you have a good chance to get your first par of the day. Is there anything more frustrating than plopping the ball some 10 or 20 yards short of the green? Now you face what is essentially the same shot—hitting the green from a short distance away. But you have wasted a stroke on a shot that in essence went nowhere.

What went wrong? First, you probably picked too weak a club: a wedge or a 9 instead of an 8 or maybe even a 7. Then, as you brought the club down, you became very aware of its short shaft and you told yourself, *"This is a weak club; I need more power."* So you brought body action into the swing. The hands and arms sensed the body action and said, *"The body's doing the work; it doesn't need us."* The arms and hands stopped working after impact and there was no extension of the arms and no proper follow-through. The shot may have taken off very nicely, climbing high in the air, but it had no "send" because there was no full follow-through. The shot landed short, necessitating a needless second approach shot.

The trouble begins when the golfer judges the distance from the ball to the green. He estimates that he is 110 yards from the pin. But the average weekend golfer, even if he shoots in the 90s or 80s, shouldn't be shooting for the pin. His target is anywhere on the green. And there may be 10 to 20 yards or more of green from the pin to the back edge of the green.

What am I saying? I am saying that he or she should estimate the distance to the target as 120 to 130 yards—not 110 yards. The golfer should select a club that will cover 120 to 130 yards, not 110 yards. That means a stronger club—the 7 or 8— and not the 9 or pitching wedge that I see most golfers use for approach shots.

But when I give this advice, golfers tell me, "But, Walter, I'll hit over the green with a stronger club."

I give them three reasons why you should opt for the stronger club rather than the one you have been using for this shot. One, on most greens, most of the trouble—water, sand traps and rough—sits in front of the green, not behind it. In short, you are nearly always better off hitting long than hitting short.

Second, if you hit "fat" with a stronger iron, you will land short of the target, true enough. But if you land only 110 yards away instead of your projected 120 to 130 yards, you will still be on the green, where you want to be. If you hit "fat" with a weaker club, you will always be short of the green.

Third, when you swing with a stronger club like the 7 or 8 for these short approach shots, there is no last-second thinking that the club is too weak for the job. There is no tendency to tell yourself, "I've got to give this a little bit extra." When you give that little bit extra on the downswing, the clubhead often comes down at too sharp an angle. The ball takes off very nicely and goes very high, but that little extra motion takes away from a full follow-through. If you don't make a full follow-through, you don't get the full distance that the club is capable of giving you.

When it comes to club selection for an approach shot, pick a club that will give you the yardage to the middle of the green plus the yardage to the back of the green. Think middle of the green *plus*, never middle of the green *minus*.

Here's one dividend you will get by selecting a

club stronger than the one you've been using for the within-120-yard approach shot. Two or three holes earlier, you swung a stronger iron and landed on the green. Now you face the same shot. You think, "I took it nice and easy with that 8-iron on that previous hole and got on the green." You have the confidence that you'll hit this green with that same iron and with that same, easy swing.

One tip about the extremely short approach shot—one about 40 yards from the green. I see many golfers take a half swing on these very short shots, bringing the clubhead up to the waist or maybe as high as the shoulders. That's fine. But as they come down, they think, "Oh-oh, I took too big a backswing." So they stop short on the follow-through, with the club only half the distance to their waist or shoulders. Again, the ball goes up, but it doesn't go very far because there was no "send" from the follow-through, and the ball lands short. If you bring the clubhead back to your waist on the backswing, bring it up to your waist on the follow-through. In any golf swing, it is important that you balance the swing and make the back end of the swing match the front end.

PRESCRIPTION: You must make the arms and hands do the work in getting the ball up and away, not the body. To impress that on your muscle memory, try this: Place a ball—a plastic one for your backyard, a real one on a range—in the middle of your stance. Stick

Place a tee in the ground a few inches in front of the ball. Strike the ball and swing through so that you also catch the tee. This will help you develop full extension of the arms, hands, and clubhead.

a tee in the ground a little past your front toe. Gripping a short iron, address the ball with a stance that is slightly more of a sitting position than normal. Most of your weight should be on the backs of your heels. Now swing as you usually do, aiming to strike the ball with a downward stroke. But swing through so that you also catch the tee. Practice this for fifteen to thirty minutes to develop extension of the arms, hands, and clubhead.

DAY FIVE

Going from Trouble to More Trouble

SYMPTOMS: Two or three strokes to get out of woods, rough, or sand.

DIAGNOSIS: Trying for the "miracle" shot that will put you on the green from the rough, fairway bunkers, or trees.

REMEDY: Swing slower and easier than the swing that landed you in trouble; choose the safest and easiest route to the fairway.

LET'S GO TO THE CLINIC: I give this as a rule of thumb for all golfers who land in trouble—and we all land in trouble a dozen times or more on any given round: Pay the penalty of one wasted stroke by putting the ball back into playing position on the fairway. If you are in the middle of trees, look for the widest and shortest route to the fairway. If that means you must chip or pitch the ball sideways to the green—or even back toward where you came from—be willing

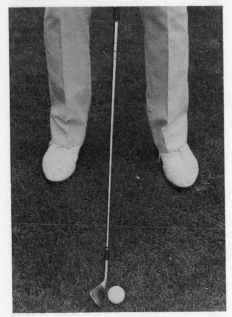

Use the most lofted club possible to get you to the fairway when hitting out of the rough.

to sacrifice distance and a stroke. Go back to the fairway, where you can get your wheels started again toward the green. If you are in a fairway bunker, pick a club with plenty of loft so you can be sure to clear the lip of the bunker, even if this means you will cover only half the distance to the green. If you are in the rough, again pick your most lofted club that will get you to the closest spot on the fairway.

But what do I see golfers do? I see them walk into the rough carrying a 4- or 5-iron. And I know what they are thinking: "The high grass is going to catch this club so I'll just take a mighty swing to cut through that grass."

We know what happens. The grass turns the club, there is only a soft impact, and the ball squirts 20 or 30 yards toward where you didn't want it to go—into more rough. Now you will have to pay two strokes to get out of trouble.

A 20-handicapper can expect to make 20 bad shots that land him in trouble on any given day. That's why he is a 20-handicapper. He can expect to be in trouble 20 times. But if he is going to take two strokes to make up for each of his 20 bad shots, he is going to find that he has become a 40-handicapper.

Having made a bad shot, the golfer tells himself that he can salvage par or a bogey with a miracle shot. Trouble is, 1) miracles are as few and far between in golf as they are anywhere else; 2) this is the worst place—in the rough, sand, or trees—to attempt to pull off a miracle shot.

I tell golfers: You are probably angry after landing in trouble. Calm down and tell yourself, "I want to make this as easy a shot as I can. I just want to chip or pitch the ball a short distance so that I am again on the fairway. That is all I want to do."

Select a lofted club that will get the ball up and out of sand or rough. As you stand over the ball—no matter where it sits—take a very slow backswing and a very slow downswing with a sharply descending arc. There should be a minimum of body move-

ment. You want to ensure that the clubhead will catch the ball cleanly. If you are in a fairway bunker (not a greenside bunker), position the ball as you would for a fairway shot—in the middle of your stance. Unlike the greenside bunker shot, where you want to hit the sand, for the fairway bunker shot you want to catch the ball cleanly—hitting the ball first, then the sand as you follow through. You want to make as high a follow-through as possible to take full advantage of the club's loft. Your thinking is fairway first, distance second.

If you are in a greenside bunker, then position the ball about even with your front heel. That's because you want to catch the sand and ball on the upswing. There should be as little body motion as possible. This is strictly a shoulder-and-arms swing, with the downswing as slow as the upswing, your eyes fixed on hitting the sand an inch or two behind the ball.

Finally, for all shots out of trouble, tell yourself before you approach the ball: "I am going to swing with half the force I used on the shot that got me here."

When in a fairway bunker, like the one I am in here, position the ball in the middle of your stance. You want to catch the ball first and then the sand (as little as possible). For a greenside bunker shot, position the ball opposite the front heel. You want to catch the sand and ball on the upswing.

PRESCRIPTION: Steer clear of trouble. If there is trouble on your left—water, sand, trees, rough—take the long way around and play all your shots to the right. On a 400-yard hole, you may have to cover 500 yards to stay out of trouble, and that will cost you a stroke. But landing just once in sand, trees, or rough will almost surely cost you a stroke, and if you land in water or out of bounds, the mistake will cost you two strokes. I can't think of a quicker way to lower your score than keeping all of your shots as far away from trouble as you can get.

DAY SIX

Failing to Make the Ends Match When You Putt

SYMPTOMS: Long putts that stop short of the hole; short putts that go too far past the hole.

DIAGNOSIS: Not following through on long putts; "stabbing" or "jabbing" at the ball on short putts.

REMEDY: Make sure that both ends of the putting stroke match up.

LET'S GO TO THE CLINIC: First of all, most golfers make putting more difficult than it really is. If you think of the putting stroke in the way I am going to describe it—the simple swinging of a pendulum—you are on your way to keeping your putting game as simple as possible and thus as error-free as possible.

Hold a putter at the end. Let the putterhead swing over the ball like a pendulum so that it swings the same distance to both sides. There is absolutely no movement of the body. That is the perfect putting stroke.

Think of the putting stroke as a pendulum that swings the same distance to one side as it does to the other side.

On long putts golfers often take the putterhead back well past their right foot. But . . .

But on the putting green I see golfers move their knees or their shoulders just before or just after impact to give the putt a little more ooomph. What happens, almost inevitably, is that this movement causes the ball to travel off line.

What I also see golfers doing on long putts is this: Facing a putt of 12 to 13 feet, they take the putterhead back nice and straight, judging that it should swing back to a point opposite the toe of their back foot. But as they come forward to impact the ball, they think: "Hey, this green looks fast, I am taking too strong a stroke." They stop the putter

. . . as they strike the ball, they worry about hitting it too hard and so stop well short of their front foot.

just after impact—and the ball rolls only 7 or 8 feet, leaving them a tough second putt.

I see the same mistake happening on short putts. Let's say the putt has to go 4 feet. Golfers will close up their stance, as they should. They bring the putter back to a point about even with the rear foot. But as they bring the putter forward, they think, "Hey, this is a short putt." They fear that a full follow-through might send the ball too far past the hole. They impact the ball—and then stop. This jabbing or stabbing stroke will almost always send

On short putts golfers shorten their stance and bring the putterhead back about even with their right foot. But . . .

. . . often on the through stroke they jab at the ball for fear of hitting it too far, stopping the putterhead short of their front foot.

the ball shooting past the hole—and now you have a three-putt green.

I can't emphasize this too much about putting: *Make the ends of the stroke match up.*

Here is what I do. I take my stance, a wider one for long putts, a narrower one for short putts. I bring the clubhead back to a point that I think is the correct length for a putt of this distance, let's say to a point opposite my right toe. Now I bring the clubhead forward and impact the ball—*and then I make sure that I continue bringing the clubhead forward until it comes to a point opposite my left toe.*

What's happened? One, I have taken a full putting stroke that will give me the distance I estimated I needed. Second, by keeping my eyes on the clubhead until it reaches the toe of my front foot, I have kept my head down, and that will give me accuracy.

When golfers ask me about putting, I usually hear at least one of these three questions:

1) What's the proper grip for putting?

I suggest the reverse-overlapping grip. It is a slight change from the overlapping grip that I suggest for most golfers when swinging a club off the tee or the fairway. To grip the putter with the reverse-overlapping grip, with the pinky of the right hand on the grip, place the forefinger of the left hand over the other fingers of the right hand. This helps to keep the clubhead from turning, and thus keeps it square on the line you want the ball to

Doing it my way: If you bring the putterhead to the back heel on the takeaway, then bring it forward to the front heel on the follow-through. Make the ends match up!

The reverse-overlapping grip for putting: With the pinky finger of the right hand on the grip, place the forefinger of the left hand over the other fingers of the right hand.

roll. The reverse-overlapping grip also helps to prevent the right hand from crossing over the left and rolling the ball off line.

Hold the club lightly with the fingers but grip it firmly with the thumbs. You should feel the clubhead through the thumb pressure. If you grip the club too tightly with the fingers and hands, there is a tendency to squeeze the club and stab at the ball.

Also, when you grip the putter, hold it at its very end so that there is no shaft showing. This increases the length of the shaft, which helps to give you the sensation that the putting swing is like all golf swings. That is, it is like the swing of a pendulum. Personally, I prefer a putter that is 36½ inches long, an inch and a half longer than a conventional man's putter, because the longer shaft gives me that feeling of a swinging pendulum.

2) Where do I position the ball?

Here we are getting into personal preferences, but I suggest placing the ball squarely between the feet in the center of the stance. The head and chin should be directly over the ball to get the pendulum effect you want. If you dropped a coin from your chin, it should plop down directly on the ball.

3) How far do I stand from the ball?

This is really up to the golfer and how he or she is built. I say: Stand where you are comfortable, even if that means leaning forward so that you are bent over the ball. The basic thing to remember about putting is the pendulum stroke. But if you can sink all of your putts with the pendulum stroke standing on your head, show me how you do it because I sure don't make them all.

I do stress this about putting: It is the great equalizer. A pro will hit the green from 150 yards out at least fifteen times out of twenty, while you may hit it only five times out of twenty. But when you and he are putting from ten feet away, if he misses he needs another stroke to hole out and if you miss, you need another stroke to hole out. And the pros as well as weekenders will miss more ten-footers than they will make.

The way I like to putt: The ball is set in the middle of the stance, and my head and chin are directly over the ball. Stand close to the ball or far away—wherever you are comfortable.

Before a practice session on the putting green, let the club swing back and forth like a pendulum. Watching the club will impress on your muscle memory how your putting stroke should look and feel, with no movement by the rest of the body.

PRESCRIPTION: Before you practice your putting, do this for five minutes: Hold the club with one hand and let it swing back and forth on its own. *Don't move your body*; let the clubhead swing by its own weight. By watching the club swinging back and forth, you will impress into your muscle memory the way your putting stroke should look and feel: a back-and-forth swinging of the arms with no movement at all by the rest of the body.

DAY SEVEN

Shifting Your Weight the Wrong Way

SYMPTOMS: Slices, hooks, topped balls, and an occasional long and straight shot from the tee.

DIAGNOSIS: Your weight is moving in the opposite direction from the direction that the clubhead is moving.

REMEDY: Always move your weight in the same direction that the clubhead is moving.

LET'S GO TO THE CLINIC: As I stand over the ball at address, I am in balance, about 50 percent of my weight on the front foot and 50 percent on the back foot. As I bring the clubhead away from the ball on the take-away, my weight moves to my back foot. It is moving in the same direction that the clubhead is traveling. I end up with about 70 percent of my weight on my back foot at the top of the backswing. As the clubhead comes down and I begin to move it toward my front side after impact, my weight shifts in the same direction that the clubhead is moving. As

On the takeaway, my weight moves toward the back foot; 70 percent of my weight is on my back foot at the top of the backswing.

After the clubhead clears my body and pulls me around, 80 percent of my weight is on my front leg, 20 percent on my back leg. The weight has shifted—during the takeaway and on the downswing and follow-through—toward the direction that the clubhead is moving.

the clubhead clears my body and pulls me around, I have about 80 percent of my weight on the front leg, about 20 percent on the back leg. In short, I have shifted my weight in the direction the clubhead is moving.

But now look at the average weekender. As the clubhead moves back to the right, toward the rear foot, I see the weight coming forward to the left side, onto the front foot. As the clubhead comes down and toward the left, or front, leg, I see the weight shifting to the right and onto the back foot. Average players too often fall away from the direction that the clubhead is moving. There is no weight behind their shots. And then they wonder why they can't hit the ball 250 yards like golfers who are half their size.

Let me be more specific. As many weekenders take the club away, they dip their front shoulder. Their weight shifts onto the front foot. Then, as the clubhead comes down, their weight recoils and shifts onto their back foot. They impact the ball with a falling-away blow and anything can happen, including a glancing impact that induces a hook spin or a slice spin. Or they top it.

Keep in mind that your weight must always move *in the same direction that the clubhead is moving.* Look carefully at the photos on pages 74–75. As the clubhead is moving away and up from the ball, my front knee, hip, and shoulder are turning in and toward the ball. At the top of my backswing, most

Wrong! Weekenders tend to dip their front shoulder on the takeaway, shifting most of the weight to the front as the clubhead moves toward the back. Then . . .

. . . as the clubhead comes down toward the front foot, the weight recoils, shifting onto the back foot. The weight has moved opposite to the direction in which the clubhead is moving.

of my weight is on my back leg and I am out of balance in the proper direction—that is, my weight has shifted in the same direction that the clubhead has moved.

As I bring the clubhead down toward the ball, I bring my weight back in balance—50 percent on each side. As the clubhead moves past my body and out toward the fairway, my weight is moving *in the same direction that the clubhead is moving*—that is, toward the target. As I finish, only the toe of my right foot is on the ground and most of my weight is on my front leg. My front knee, hip, and shoulder are turned toward where the ball is going—not turned toward where the ball was. I have made a complete weight shift, first to the back foot, then to the front foot, the weight always going toward where the clubhead is going.

I am often asked this question: "Should I lift my front heel on the takeaway? I see all the pros lift their heel."

I lift my left heel on most tee shots and most fairway shots. Nearly all pros do. But I tell high-handicappers and even most golfers with handicaps higher than 10: Keep the left heel on the ground.

Here's why: If you allow the left heel to come up two inches, the clubhead will come up two inches higher at the top of the backswing than if you had kept the heel on the ground (as it was at address). You must remember to bring the clubhead down

At the finish most of my weight is on the front foot, only the toe of the back foot is on the ground. Front shoulder, hip, and knee face toward the target.

those two inches so the clubhead meets the ball as squarely as it faced the ball at address. The pros remember to bring the clubhead down; most weekenders do not. So keep that front heel down and just turn the front ankle, knee, hip, and shoulder so that they angle in toward the ball, not to a point ahead of the ball.

PRESCRIPTION: Place a ball on the ground in the middle of your stance. Stand over the ball without a club in your hands. Put your hands on your hips and turn the left ankle, knee, elbow, and shoulder so that the left elbow is pointing directly at the ball. You can't do this exercise with a club in your hands, but practice it to impress on your muscle memory shifting your weight to the back side. Then turn the right ankle, knee, hip, and shoulder so that the right elbow is pointing directly at the ball. Do this for fifteen minutes at a time and you will get the feeling of always moving your weight in the same direction the clubhead is moving—first to the right, then to the left.

Or try this exercise if you are supple enough: Place a club behind your back horizontally at waist level so that the shaft is gripped by both of your bent elbows. The clubhead points toward the target, and the club's grip points away from the target. Place both hands on your hips as you face the ball centered between your feet.

Turn, simulating the upswing. The clubhead should point to a spot above the ball. Now, turn and simulate the downswing. The club's grip should point to a spot above the ball. Practice this for 20-minute stretches as often as you can before your next session.

DAY EIGHT

"Slow-Smash" Rhythm and Tempo

SYMPTOMS: Hooks and slices; occasionally, a 50-yard approach shot that goes 50 yards over the green, leaving you to face another 50-yard approach shot back to the green.

DIAGNOSIS: The downswing is almost twice as fast as the upswing.

REMEDY: A slightly faster upswing so that it comes closer to matching the speed of the downswing.

LET'S GO TO THE CLINIC: A good golf swing should have the same pace from beginning to end; otherwise, the rhythm is herky-jerky instead of smooth. Bring the clubhead up at, say, thirty miles per hour. You should bring the clubhead down at no more than thirty-five to thirty-seven miles per hour (since it is only natural to speed up going downhill). Follow through at the same thirty-five to thirty-seven miles per hour.

When some golfers take a practice swing, they

bring the club down at about the same speed that they used to bring the club up. But when they step up to swing for real, both low- and high-handicappers often take the club back nice and slow and under control at thirty-five miles per hour, but then they bring it down to the ball at forty-five to fifty miles per hour and sometimes even faster.

That is a swing of power and speed only; it is not a swing that is under control. It is a swing that you could label "slow" on the upswing, "smash" on the downswing. Slow-smash swings are as out of control as a car without a driver. When an out-of-control clubhead smashes a ball, it can do the same kind of damage that an out-of-control car can do to a crowd of pedestrians. Almost anything can and will go wrong.

I like to ask golfers who suffer from the slow-smash syndrome, "What is your favorite club?"

Most will say a 6-iron or one of the more lofted utility woods, like the ginty, which is a 7-wood. They get good results with a club like the 7-wood because it is bottom-weighted, for one thing, and it gets into the grass deeper to contact the bottom of the ball. You get the kind of high, soaring shots that give you confidence, so naturally a club like the ginty is often a favorite.

I ask a golfer to swing at three or four balls with his or her favorite club. Most will swing the club very smoothly and hit nice high shots. They have so much confidence in their favorite club that they will come down with the club at approximately the same speed that they used to bring the club up.

Now, when I give the golfer a different club and ask him or her to swing at a few balls, the golfer swings like a different person, with a much more aggressive and quicker downswing. As a result, the swing is out of synch, and the shot goes agley, as the Scots say.

Again, I ask the golfer to swing at three or four balls with the favorite club—and again the downswing is slow, the swing is in synch, and most of the shots are high and toward the target.

Once more I hand the golfer the other club. But this time I say, "Let's pretend we didn't switch clubs. Let's pretend you are still swinging with your favorite club. Give me that same confident tempo on the downswing that you gave me when you swung your favorite club."

Sometimes I get results right away, sometimes not for a while. But most golfers get the message: You should swing all clubs at the same rate going down that you employed going up. Let the club do the job, the same job you let the club do when you swung easily with a favorite club and got all those pretty shots.

Count on the club doing the work, not the force of your swing.

PRESCRIPTION: I will sometimes suggest that golfers take the club up at a slightly faster speed than normal. Now

Bring both clubs down at the same pace you usually use on your downswing.

The two clubs crack together when you speed up the downswing so that the trailing club in your right hand catches up with the leading club in your left.

they will be closer to matching the pace of the downswing, and the swing will be smoother in its pace. But I emphasize: "Don't also add speed to the downswing, or you'll be back where you started—a swing that is out of synch."

Here is a drill that can impress on your muscle memory what it feels like to match the speed of the downswing with the speed of the upswing:

Select two clubs. Grip one, a long iron like the 3 or 4, in your left hand, and a short iron like the 9 in your right hand. Bring both clubs back as you usually do on your upswing—nice and easy and slow. Now bring both clubs down at the same speed you usually bring down a club during a downswing. Chances are the two clubs will crack together because you have speeded up the swing so that the trailing club in your right hand catches up with the leading club in your left hand.

What should happen is that the downswing pace matches the pace of the upswing. The two clubs should stay the same distance apart on the downswing that they were on the upswing. When you bring both clubs down so that they are the same distance apart at impact as they were at address,

When the clubs are the same distance apart throughout the swing—the same distance that they were at address—you have matched the speed of the downswing with the speed of the upswing.

you know you are matching exactly the speed of the downswing with the speed of the upswing. Practice that for periods of ten or fifteen minutes. You will get the feeling of a truly rhythmic golf swing—one end, the upswing, matching the other end, the downswing.

Choosing the Wrong Club for Par-3 Tee Shots

SYMPTOMS: Tee shots that land short of the green or fly left or right.

DIAGNOSIS: Trying to force too much yardage out of a weak club.

REMEDY: Keep in mind that a club that can send the ball 150 yards on the fairway is probably not the club you should use to tee off on a 150-yard par-3 hole.

LET'S GO TO THE CLINIC: Club selection can sometimes seem like a kind of black-magic mystery, but by remembering two simple things you can make club selection simple when you tee off on par 3s. First, on most par 3s, you are nearly always better off hitting long rather than short. Trouble is usually in front of the green, less often behind the green. Second, when you grip an 8-iron rather than a 7 or a 6, the shorter shaft gives you the feeling that the club is weak; you also crouch lower with an 8 than you do

91

with a longer club like a 7 or a 6. That, too, gives you a sense of the club being weak.

So what happens? You put power and force into the swing, and power and force mean a bad swing, with the body coming around too soon. Result: The clubhead comes across the line of intended flight and you hook or slice.

This is probably the most important thing to remember as you stand on the tee of a par-3 hole. Let's say the hole is 150 yards long. The iron, say a 7, that covers 150 yards for you from a fairway to a green is probably not the club you should select for this tee shot.

Why?

Because you are teeing up the ball for this shot. The ball is already in the air. When you swing from the fairway, you are hitting a ball that is on the ground. When you contact a ball that is teed up, you will get more height than you would if the ball were on the ground. And that height will cost you distance; hence, you need a stronger club for this 150-yard tee shot than you would need for a 150-yard fairway shot.

When you face a par-3 tee shot (the most demanding shot in golf for a reason I will explain in a moment), you must consider whether you must cover water or traps in front of the green, whether the green is elevated, and whether the pin is located at the front or the back of the green. And again I remind you: It is nearly always better to be a little bit long than a lot short or a lot left or right.

Two wrongs are shown here as I swing from the tee of a par-3 hole. One, I am applying too much power and force to the swing; the left side of my body is coming around too soon. Result: a hook or slice. Two, I am not teeing up the ball. If the rules allow you to put the ball into the air even before you swing, take advantage of the rule.

That means, of course, selecting a stronger club than you would normally use for the distance, a 7 instead of an 8. When you select a club that you are positive will cover the yardage—and maybe more— you take a smooth and easy swing, leaving out the body action that causes hooks and slices.

Finally, many golfers get confused when they choose a weaker club rather than a stronger club for par-3 tee shots. They remember to take a nice smooth swing, but since they lose distance because the ball is teed up, they land short of the green. And that leaves them bewildered. "This is a 160-yard par-3 and I landed short, Walter, but on the last hole I used this club to go 160 yards. What did I do wrong?"

They forgot about that teed-up ball.

PRESCRIPTION: On most par-3 holes, especially ones where there is trouble in the front of the green and none behind, choose one club stronger than one you would normally use for the distance. And if the wind is blowing in your face or if the green is elevated with the pin toward the back, choose a club that's two clubs stronger: a 6-iron instead of an 8, for example. And banish the fear of so many golfers: "I don't want to overshoot the green." Being a little bit long is better than being a little bit short, especially if being short puts you into a trap.

Use this strategy: On long par-3 holes, ones that are 190 yards plus, think about laying up short with

On a long par-3 hole, think about laying up short in a comfort zone. A pitch from there can land you close enough to the pin for a par 3 or a bogey 4—a "par" on a hole of this caliber.

a favorite club in a "comfort zone." That is an area in the fairway short of the green, either to its left or right or directly in front, that leaves you with a 40- or 50-yard pitch-and-run shot. From that short distance, you might pitch close enough to the pin for a one-putt and par. But even if you have to two-putt to hole out, a bogey 4 is a good score on a par-3 hole of this caliber.

Remember that a tee shot on a par-3 hole is golf's most demanding shot. From a relatively long distance, you are being asked to drop the ball close enough to the pin, within 30 feet, so that you can hole out in two putts. No other tee shot demands that kind of accuracy to that tight a landing area.

DAY TEN

Slicing

SYMPTOMS: Shots that trace a banana-shape curve from the golfer's left to the golfer's right, with the ball spinning back toward the golfer.

DIAGNOSIS: An outside-inside swing.

REMEDY: At impact the left hip must face straight toward the line of flight and the ball; and the left arm must be as straight at impact as it was at address.

LET'S GO TO THE CLINIC: Ninety to 95 percent of all golfers slice. Many, if not most, slice because they start their downswing with the lower gear—the knees and hips—instead of the upper gear—the arms and shoulders. This causes the left side to turn toward the target much too soon. At impact the left hip is turning toward the target instead of being where it belongs: facing the ball and the line of flight.

Another reason why most golfers slice: Most golfers are right-handed. Because their right arm is stronger and dominant, the right side pushes the left arm out of the way on the downswing, causing it

At impact the left hip must face the line of flight and the left arm must be as straight as it was at address.

The body is turning too soon. At impact the left hip is facing toward the target, opening the clubface and spinning the ball to the golfer's right.

to bend instead of straighten and form a V with the right arm at impact. With the left arm bent, the clubhead impacts the ball with an open face, spinning the ball left to right.

Let's go over this again. It's important: If the left hip is facing the target or the left elbow is pointing to the target at impact, the clubhead comes at the ball from the outside to the inside of the target line (the line from ball to target). This outside-inside path means that the clubface is open when it impacts the ball. And an open clubface at impact puts a slicing spin on the ball. The slice can be a wicked one if the left elbow is bent *and* the left hip is facing toward the target.

To summarize, there are two basic swing faults that cause a slice: 1) starting the downswing with the lower gear instead of the upper gear (this causes the left hip to turn too soon toward the target); 2) allowing the right side to overpower the left side and bend the left arm. When you commit either of these two faults, the club impacts the ball with a glancing outside-inside blow that imparts the slicing, left-to-right spin. When you commit both faults at the same time, you have a humongous slice.

Lots of golfers who slice try to erase the error by aiming to the left of the target. They also swing harder and faster to try to get more distance, making up for the distance they lose because a sliced ball spins backward, toward the golfer.

The left arm is bent at impact, the elbow pointing toward the target and causing the clubhead to impact the ball from outside the target line to inside the target line, imparting a slicing spin.

They commit two wrongs—aiming wrong and swinging harder. In golf's quirky way, the two wrongs sometimes make a right. The ball curves left-to-right and hits the target—and the extra force of the swing adds distance that makes up for the distance lost because of the slice's backward spin.

That is not always an effective solution, however. Sometimes, when golfers aim left and swing hard, everything comes together in their swing and they hit the ball straight—but to a point far left of the target and 30 yards too long. And then they howl, "Holy mackerel, a straight ball got me into trouble!"

The purpose of this book is not to teach you how two wrongs can make a right. Let me teach you how two rights can make a third right—straight balls instead of slices. The two rights are keeping the left hip facing the ball at impact, and the left arm as straight at impact as it was at address.

PRESCRIPTION: I see most golfers do the right thing on the upswing—that is, their arms and shoulders bring the clubhead back and up. I have never seen a golfer, even a beginner, start the upswing by turning the hips and knees. But when I see golfers who slice, I see them start the downswing by turning their hips and knees. If the arms and shoulders started the backswing, the arms and shoulders should start the downswing. They should be followed—as they were on the backswing—by the hips and knees. The upper gear should start the upswing and the downswing.

To impress on your muscle memory the need to keep the left hip facing the ball and straight with the line of flight until after impact, try this:

At a practice range, swing at balls with your feet and legs close together. This very weak stance takes most of the strength away from the lower gear and forces you to keep the left hip straight with the line of flight. Hit about a dozen balls with the feet close together and you will see the ball go straight. Then, continue to swing at balls, gradually moving the feet wider apart until they are the normal shoulder-width. But continue to trust the arms and hands to lead the way, the hips following after impact, and you will see balls going straight, the slice beginning to fly out of your life.

Here's a drill to build left-arm response—that is, to teach the left arm to lead the right side. Grip the club by its neck with the left hand and simulate address and a full takeaway, the left shoulder touching the chin. Then come all the way down with the club, swinging through an imaginary ball and continuing into a full and high follow-through. You will build left-arm response to the rest of the swing, the left arm folding at the top of the upswing, but straightening again as it comes down into the impact zone.

One Final Prescription: Making Your Game Mentally Right

I don't want to leave you without looking briefly at some of the mental mistakes I see golfers make most often. "Course management" is a fancy phrase used by pros when we talk strategy, but what we really mean is that you should think before you swing. The golfer who thinks before swinging can nearly always turn in a lower score than a mechanically superior golfer who doesn't think before swinging—as I will prove to you.

THE FIVE MOST COMMON MENTAL MISTAKES

1. Forgetting that on every hole there is one shot—what I call the critical shot—that the smart golfer makes easy and pressure-free.

The critical shot on a par-3 hole for the low-to-medium-handicapper (one who averages around 95) is the shot from the tee. You must land that shot within 25 to 30 feet of the pin to have any appreciable chance at scoring par. If you average above 95, the critical shot is the second shot, the approach shot that has to land you close enough to the pin for two putts and a bogey 4. That bogey 4 is "par" to a player of your caliber.

The critical shot on a par-4 hole for the low-to-medium-handicapper is the second shot. That's the shot the golfer must land on the green to have a chance at a birdie or a par 4. For the high-handicapper, the critical shot is the third shot, the shot that must reach the green to give you a chance at your "par" 5.

The critical shot on a par-5 hole for the below-95 golfer is the third shot. It's the shot that must come close enough to the pin for two putts and a par 5. For the high-handicapper, the critical shot is the fourth shot, the one that must put you close enough to the hole for a "par" 6.

Now let's see why too many weekenders don't make those critical shots easy and pressure-free.

Many low-handicappers, facing that critical first shot on a par 3, will not tee up the ball. Golf is a tough enough game without your making it harder by not taking full advantage of the rules. And if the rules allow you to put the ball into the air before you swing, take advantage of the rule. With the ball teed up, perhaps as much as half of the job is done. Now all you need to do is send it straight and the proper distance. Make the critical shot as easy as you can.

On a long par-3, one that's more than 175 yards, the high-handicapper must think of his second shot as the critical shot. But I see high-handicappers trying to hit a ball 200 yards from tee to a par-3 green. They will hit a ball that far with accuracy maybe once in 50 tries. In trying to cover those 200 yards, they swing too fast and too hard. By now I don't have to tell you what happens next. More likely than not, the golfer hooks or slices into sand or rough and is lucky to end up with a double-bogey 5.

On the long par-3s, I tell high-handicappers to aim for the comfort zone. That's a fairway area free of trouble, usually in front of the green and to its left or right. From there, only 30 or 40 yards away, you can aim a pitch-and-run shot at the pin. Pitch a ball about halfway to the pin on the fly, then let it roll across the green the other half of the way. Hitting to a target from about 40 yards away is a lot easier than trying to hit the same target from 200 yards away. It's a comfort, pressure-free shot that can drop the ball close enough to the pin for a two-putt and your "par" 4. For a high-handicapper, a bogey 4 on a par-3 hole of this difficulty is an excellent score.

On short-to-medium-length par-4 holes, the medium- or high-handicapper will probably get the tee shot out about 175 to 190 yards. Now the golfer faces a shot of 200 yards or less to the green. Too often the temptation is to go for it with a Sunday punch shot. The golfer selects a 3-wood and says, "I will swing a little harder and a little stronger." Swinging harder and stronger nearly always spells trouble.

For both medium- and high-handicappers, after a tee shot of 175 to 190 yards, the smart move is to set up a third, comfort shot. For this second shot, take a lofted wood, like a 7 or the popular ginty wood. You are looking for only 150 to 160 yards, so swing nice and easy, aiming for the corner of the green that is free of traps.

This easy swing should bring you to within 40 yards of the green. Now, for the third, critical shot, you face a wide-open green with nothing in front of you except the pin. You can pick your favorite short iron. In short, it should be a comfortable shot. You pitch—or pitch and run—the ball to the green. From this distance you should land within 20 to 30 feet of the hole, close enough for two putts and your "par" 5.

On par-5 holes, most medium- and high-handicappers are content with their first three shots to eat up distance to the green, about 530 yards away. The critical shot is the fourth. Make this shot as easy and pressure-free as possible.

Let's say you are 80 yards from the pin after three shots. Up to now you have not been too concerned about accuracy, trying only to keep the ball somewhere in the middle of a fairway that may be as wide as 100 yards.

But now the fairway funnels down to perhaps a width of only 40 yards as it comes into the green. More likely than not, there are bunkers on either side of that narrow 40-yard neck of fairway. The accuracy tolerance has been cut in half. Yet now, when accuracy is suddenly more important than it was on the three previous shots, golfers put even more pressure on themselves by aiming for the pin as they try to squeeze the ball through that narrow neck of fairway.

Wrong! And here's why: Most golfers don't allow for the space at the back of the green (when the pin is set in the middle or the front of the green). By using this space, you have more than doubled your target landing area. And as I have said earlier in this book, trouble nearly always waits in front or at the sides of greens, not nearly as often at the back of greens. You are nearly always better off hitting past the pin than hitting short of the pin. Take a stronger club than you would normally take for this distance and then take an easy, relaxed, slowed-down swing. But remember to make *a full follow-through.* Even if your shot rolls past the pin, you are still on the green. You have taken an easy, comfortable swing and made this critical shot as pressure-free as possible. Chances are, you will get your bogey 6, which is "par" for you.

Don't let the term bogey become a mental boogeyman. What would your score be if you bogeyed every hole on a par-72 course? It would be 72 plus 18 and that adds up to 90, a darn good score for any amateur, especially a weekender.

2. Forgetting that a pitch to a green over sand is a "no hurry" kind of shot.

Few mental mistakes will cost you more strokes than landing 10 feet short of a sand trap and then, trying to hit over the sand to the green, landing in the trap.

I tell golfers to remind themselves before this shot: "The ball may have been in a hurry to go the 300 or 400 or 500 yards to come within 20 yards of this green. But now it should be in no hurry to go such a short distance. So why should you hurry it along?"

But weekenders do hurry it along with a fast and hard downswing. But as they impact the ball, they say to themselves, "Hey, this is a short shot, I don't want the ball to go too far." So they stop and do not follow through. They punch the ball. They catch the ball at the equator and hit a line drive that either catches the lip and bounces back into the sand or flies to the other side of the green, perhaps into another bunker.

I tell golfers: "Think of this shot as an underhanded toss to the green. How would you toss the ball underhanded to the green? You would bring back your arm slowly, lob the ball to carry over the lip of the bunker, and follow through so your arm is high—the hand reaching as high as the lip of the bunker—to make sure the ball floats in a high arc and lands softly on the green."

Think of your swing for this shot—with a pitching wedge or a sand wedge—as being an underhanded toss.

3. The "Texas Wedge" mistake

In Texas and other parts of the Sunbelt, where the grass on the fringes of greens is burnt to thin or nonexistent, golfers will often use the "Texas wedge," their putter, and putt the ball through the thin grass from as far away as six feet off the green. That may work fine in Texas, but if your ball lands in lush grass on the fringe, taking a favorite club like the putter and trying to putt the ball to the green is nearly always a mistake. The thick grass offers too much resistance and the ball will usually slow up too much to roll to the cup. Or, if you hit the ball too hard, the ball will bounce over the grass, go off line, and then roll too fast over the green, going past the cup. In short, when you putt from thick grass, you have little control over the speed and direction of the putt.

My rule of thumb is this: If you are a foot—or perhaps two feet—off the rim of the green, consider using a putter to nudge the ball onto the green and toward the cup, especially if the grass is thin and cut low. But two feet would be my absolute maximum. If the ball is more than 24 inches off the green, use a lofted iron to pitch the ball onto the green where it can roll smoothly toward the cup.

4. Overcharging your putts

You land on the green in three strokes and your ball rests about 18 feet from the cup. Even though this may have been one of the most accurate approach shots you ever hit, coming from about 100 yards to within 18 feet, no golfer is ever satisfied. As you walk onto the green, you tell yourself, "If I had just caught that ball a little fuller and gotten a little more altitude, the ball would have landed no more than 10 feet from the pin."

Nor are most golfers ever satisfied with a bogey 5 when they think they should have scored a par 4 on a hole. And right now, the ball only 18 feet from the cup, the temptation is very strong to go for the par. You are thinking about charging straight at the cup, even though the odds are very much against your sinking the putt. What happens, far more often than not, is that the putt rolls 6 or 8 feet past the hole. Now you need two more strokes to hole out. Instead of a par, you walk away from a three-putt green with a double-bogey.

On a putt of more than 10 feet, I tell weekend golfers: "Coax the ball into a circle no more than two feet from the cup. Then you are close to guaranteeing that you will hole out in two putts, which is all that is expected of you."

Should you be aggressive when you putt? Yes, absolutely, but charge for the hole only on putts 10 feet and under. For the player with a handicap of 22 or higher, it is a mistake to be aggressive on putts longer than 10 feet. All that aggression will only make you an even higher-handicap golfer.

5. Boneheads on the doglegs

On both long and short doglegs, I see golfers make the same basic mistake: They go toward the dogleg instead of going away from the dogleg.

Let's assume the dogleg is a 450-yard par 4 with the dogleg to the right. Many high-handicappers will aim their tee shots at the middle of the fairway or to the right, where the hole bends. Let's suppose they hit a good tee shot and land about 180 to 190 yards out on the right side (they are likely to be on the right since 90 percent of high-handicappers slice).

They may be congratulating themselves until they get to their ball and see what they face: trees that line the bend of the hole. The trees block any direct shot at the green. They must now waste a shot by hitting to the left side of the fairway so that the next shot can be an approach shot to the green.

They would have been much better off aiming the tee shot to the left side, even if that added 20 or

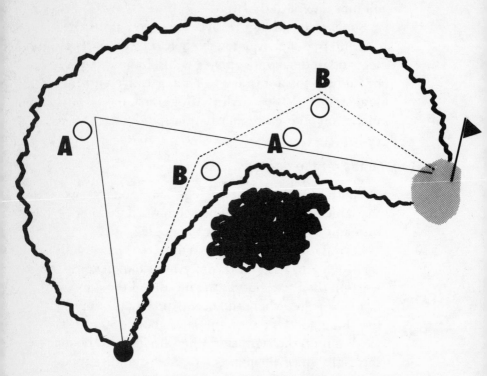

On holes like this, playing away from the dogleg, as A is doing, is a smarter strategy than playing close to the dogleg, as B is doing. B's second shot to the green is blocked by trees at the bend of the dogleg. B must play the second shot to the middle of the fairway. A has an open fairway to get to the green in three, the same as B, but without risk.

30 yards to the length of the hole. Now, for the second shot, they have a clear and open road to the green, which they can reach with their third shot, no trouble blocking the way.

On the short doglegs—say a par 4 of about 380 yards—the weekender is sorely tempted to get greedy and bite off a little more yardage. I see golfers trying to fly tee shots over trees at the dogleg or trying to skirt the corner by landing the tee shot close to the rough.

Two things can happen—and both are bad. If you slice more than usual, you will land deep in the trees. You may need two or three strokes just to get back on the fairway. And even if you land in the fairway on the right side, you must hit a low punch shot to duck under the trees and reach the fairway. Again, if the ball slices just a trifle, you will be making your next shot from deep in the woods.

And what have you accomplished by trying to bite 30 or 40 yards off this short hole? You still need two shots to get to the green whether you aim at the dogleg or away from it.

You can see why. If you aim the tee shot away from the dogleg, the ball will land on the left side, out about 170 yards. Now you are looking at a 210-yard shot to the green compared to a 180-yard shot if you had landed to the right. But on the right side, you can't go for the green because the route is blocked. You must waste the second shot, then go for the green on the third shot. On the left side, you can take an easy, pressure-free shot and lay up short of the green, then aim for the pin with a pitch-and-run shot. You are on the green in three, the same as the golfer who took so many risks to his or her scoring health—but got no reward.

To sum up the mental side of golf: Think, then swing.

Off on Your Own: Be Sure to Take Advantage of the Rules

Knowing the rules, as we made clear in our first book, *Break 100 in 21 Days*, can save you strokes. Unfortunately, too many golfers think they know the rules—but they don't understand them completely, which is almost as bad as not understanding them at all. These are the five most common misunderstandings about rules that I encounter:

1. Failing to understand the difference between match play and stroke play

In match play the penalty for an infraction is often the loss of one hole. In stroke play, it is a one-stroke or two-stroke penalty added to your score.

2. Carrying too many clubs in your bag

You are only allowed to carry a maximum of fourteen clubs during any round. Accidentally carrying an extra putter, for example, will cost you two strokes per hole per extra club—but the penalty cannot exceed two holes.

3. Failing to take distance as a penalty after hitting out of bounds or losing a ball

After hitting a ball out of bounds or losing it in the rough or trees (you are allowed five minutes to look for it), most weekenders will drop a new ball, give themselves a one-stroke penalty (so that they lie two), and then hit their third shot from the spot where the ball went out of bounds or was lost.

That's wrong. There is also a distance penalty involved. You must go back to where you hit the first ball and hit a new ball, counting that swing as your third stroke. (The original stroke was the first, the penalty stroke was the second.)

To speed play, golfers should hit a provisional ball when they hit a ball they think might be out of bounds or lost. If the first ball is indeed out of bounds or lost, they can then play the provisional ball, that swing being their fourth stroke. If the original ball is neither lost in a water hazard nor out of bounds, the player shall abandon the provisional ball and continue to play with the original ball.

4. Incorrectly dropping the ball after landing in a water hazard or under trees

I don't know whether or not they do it on purpose, but I see many weekenders playing a little cute when they drop a ball after landing in water, or after they declare an unplayable lie.

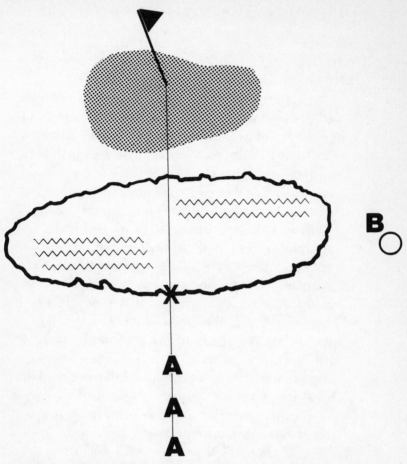

When you hit into water, you may drop a ball near the spot where the ball crossed into the hazard. You must drop the ball along a line directly between the hole and the spot where the ball is dropped. But the spot must be behind the water hazard, keeping the point at which the original ball last crossed the margin of the water hazard directly between the hole and the spot where the ball is to be dropped. There is no limit as to how far behind the water hazard the ball may be dropped. Too many golfers mistakenly drop the ball in an area (like B) where they no longer have to cross the hazard.

Let's look at the water hazard first. I see golfers drop the ball to the left or right of the water; now they no longer have to clear the hazard.

That is very much a no-no. The rule is quite clear. Determine at what point the ball crossed from land into water and what the line of flight was. Taking a one-stroke penalty, you may drop the ball anywhere you like—*as long as you place it farther away from the green than where it hit the water and on the same line that the ball was traveling when it crossed into the water.*

When a ball lands under a tree whose limbs stick out and prevent a golf swing, you may declare an unplayable lie. That's all right, as long as you inform your playing partners and take a one-stroke penalty. But what's wrong is what some do next. They crawl under the limbs and move the ball to a spot to the left or right of the tree that is blocking your line to the green.

Again, a no-no. You are allowed to move the ball only two club lengths from the spot where it landed in the unplayable lie. And you must move it away from the green, not toward the green.

Now if that still leaves you with an unplayable lie—you are still stuck under the tree—you can continue to move the ball away from the green. *But you must keep the ball on the same line that the ball was traveling when it struck the tree. In short, you must still clear the tree or play around it.*

If you deem that impossible or impractical, you can take the ball back where you last hit it and swing again, now giving up both a stroke and distance.

5. Touching your club to the sand while getting ready to blast or hit out of a bunker

The rules strictly forbid a golfer from touching the sand before he or she swings at a ball in a bunker. (During the swing for a blast shot, of course, you must contact the sand, but that happens *during* the swing.) There are at least two reasons for this rule: 1) touching the sand with your club could make an indentation that would give you a more favorable lie; 2) touching the sand helps you determine the hardness of the sand, which is an unfair advantage.

You may take a practice swing as long as you don't touch the sand anywhere in the bunker.

Twelve "Nutshell" Tips for Keeping Your Golf Game Healthy Forever

Most pros say that if you can go through a round of golf and not once make an error that you usually make—like, for example, going from one trouble spot to another trouble spot—you will shave at least one stroke off your game, perhaps two or three. So if, with practice, you can stop making at least five of the ten most common errors in golf during any one round of golf, your score is going to drop anywhere from five to ten strokes. The 100 golfer becomes a 90 golfer, the 90 golfer becomes an 80 golfer, the 80 golfer explores that wonderful world of the 70s.

You can come in with such scores by keeping in mind these twelve "nutshell" tips when you practice and play:

1. Always bring your palms toward the club from the sides, not from the top or bottom, gripping the club so that the palms face each other. Hold the club, don't squeeze or choke it. And take a stance that's in balance, 50 percent of your weight on one side, 50 percent on the other side. The head and chin should be on a plumb line over the ball.

2. Keep in mind that all tee shots are position shots, not distance shots. You want to position the ball anywhere on the fairway (or on the green on short par 3s) in the 175-yard-or-longer range.

3. Do not cross the intended line of flight—the line between the ball and target—with your hands or the clubhead. Think of a roller-coaster track running from ball to target. Keep your hands and the clubhead rising and falling and rising again while always on the track.

4. Put "legs" on approach shots—don't leave them short—by remembering on the follow-through to keep the left arm working "overtime." It must not quit at impact. The left arm must continue the swing past the front leg, reaching out and trying to "shake hands" with the target.

5. When you land in trouble—sand, rough, trees—tell yourself: "I will take the shortest and widest route to safety, no matter where that may be in relation to the green. And I will take an easy swing, not a fast or hard swing, because a fast or hard swing is probably what got me here. In short, I will swing slower than I did on that last blankety-blank shot."

6. As you stand over a putt, remind yourself that you have not completed the putt until your putterhead passes the point in the through swing that it reached in the backswing. If the putterhead

reached your back toe in the backswing, it must reach your front toe in the follow-through. And do not look up until you see the putterhead reach that front toe.

7. As you take the clubhead back, shift your weight to the right. As the clubhead comes down and through the ball, shift your weight to the left. Your weight is always moving in the same direction that the clubhead is moving.

8. Take the clubhead back and up at, for example, thirty miles per hour; bring it back down and through only a little faster—at no more than thirty-two to thirty-five miles per hour. Obey "the thirty-five-mile-per-hour speed law."

9. Think strong when teeing off on par-3 holes. Use the firepower of a stronger club than you would normally use for the distance; don't try to employ body action to get more distance with a weaker club. If you use a 7-iron to go 150 yards on the fairway, use a 6-iron on a 150-yard par-3 hole, a 5-iron if the wind is blowing in your face or the green is elevated.

10. To get the slice out of your life, take the clubhead up and bring the clubhead down on a line that is "on track"—that is, on the intended line of flight. Keep the left arm straight at impact and keep the left hip facing the ball until after impact.

11. Know on each hole how to make your "critical" shot your "comfort" shot.

12. Make sure you understand the rules that cost you strokes, as well as the rules that can save you strokes.

Remember these twelve tips and say hello to your healthy new game—a game cured of the physical and mental maladies that made it sickly for too long.

About the Authors

Walter Ostroske has been a PGA Teaching Pro for the past twenty-five years. He has played in numerous tournaments and has written magazine articles on golf instruction. Currently head pro at the Hempstead Golf and Country Club on Long Island, he is a member of the MacGregor Advisory Staff.

John Devaney is the author of more than twenty-five books and has written hundreds of magazine articles on sports. The former editor of *Sport Magazine*, he is the editor of Harris Publications golf magazines and is an adjunct lecturer at Fordham University.

Walter Ostroske and John Devaney are the authors of the highly successful *Break 100 in 21 Days: A How-to Guide for the Weekend Golfer*.

ABOUT THE PHOTOGRAPHER

Aime La Montagne is a successful free-lance photographer living in Palmer, Massachusetts. His golfing photographs have appeared in national magazines.

Trying to help you out of trouble (left to right): John Devaney, Walter Ostroske, Aime La Montagne.

These books are available at your local bookstore or wherever books are sold. Ordering is also easy and convenient. Just call 1-800-631-8571 or send your order to:

The Putnam Publishing Group
390 Murray Hill Parkway, Dept. B
East Rutherford, NJ 07073

____ Break 100 in 21 Days	399-51600-X	$8.95	$11.75
____ Correct the 10 Most Common Golf Problems in 10 Days	399-51656-5	8.95	11.75
____ Two-Putt Greens in 18 Days	399-51747-2	8.95	11.75
____ Golf Games Within the Game	399-51762-6	8.95	11.75
____ The Whole Golf Catalog	399-51623-9	15.95	20.95
____ Golf Rules in Pictures	399-51438-4	7.95	10.50
____ Golf Techniques in Pictures	399-51664-6	7.95	10.50

Subtotal $_____

Postage and handling* $_____

Sales tax (CA, NJ, NY, PA) $_____

Total Amount Due $_____

Payable in U.S. funds (no cash orders accepted). $10.00 minimum for credit card orders.
*Postage and handling: $2.00 for 1 book, 50¢ for each additional book up to a maximum of $4.50.

Enclosed is my ☐ check ☐ money order
Please charge my ☐ Visa ☐ MasterCard ☐ American Express

Card # _____ Expiration date _____

Signature as on charge card _____

Name _____

Address _____

City _____ State _____ Zip _____

Please allow six weeks for delivery. Prices subject to change without notice.